D1377443

JIM THORPE

by
Wayne Coffey

BLACKBIRCH PRESS, INC.
Woodbridge, Connecticut

Published by Blackbirch Press, Inc.
One Bradley Road
Woodbridge, CT 06525

©1993 Blackbirch Press, Inc.
First Edition

Manufactured in the United States of America
10 9 8 7 6 5 4 3 2 1

Editor: Bruce Glassman
Photo Research: Grace How
Illustrations: David Taylor

Library of Congress Cataloging-in-Publication Data

Coffey, Wayne R.
   Jim Thorpe / by Wayne Coffey. — 1st ed.
       p.   cm. — (Olympic gold!)
   Includes bibliographical references and index.
   Summary: Biography of one of the greatest athletes of all
time, Jim Thorpe.
   ISBN 1-56711-005-3
   1.Thorpe, Jim, 1887–1953—Juvenile literature.
2. Athletes—United States—Biography—Juvenile literature.
[1. Thorpe, Jim, 1887–1953. 2. Athletes. 3. Indians of North
America—Biography.] I. Title. II.Series.
GV697.T5C64 1993
796'.092—dc20
[B]   92-21230
                                      CIP
                                      AC

Contents

1

The Beginning of a Legend

There wasn't anything Jim Thorpe couldn't do.

I n 1950, sportswriters from the Associated Press conducted a nation-wide survey to answer this question: Who is the greatest male athlete of the first half of the twentieth century? There was quite a list to choose from. Was it the legendary Babe Ruth? Was it Red Grange, the first big star of the National Football League? What about the blazing hero of Berlin, Jesse Owens, who won four gold medals in the 1936 Olympics?

When the votes were counted, the results were overwhelmingly in favor of one man. The winner was Jim Thorpe. A Native American from Oklahoma, Jim was awarded 262 votes. The total number of votes given to everyone else was 141.

Opposite:
Many people who saw Jim Thorpe on the football field believed he was the greatest player of all time.

The lopsided voting in the poll wasn't an insult to the accomplishments of Ruth, Owens, or anyone else. It was simply a tribute to a man who was as close to Superman as any human being could be. There wasn't anything Jim Thorpe couldn't do. He jumped high. He ran fast. His strength and power were extraordinary, as was his agility.

New Kid on the Field

Jim Thorpe first achieved athletic stardom at the Carlisle School in Carlisle, Pennsylvania. Shortly after he arrived there, he came upon several large, well-muscled athletes working out by the track. The young men were throwing the hammer. The hammer is a 16-pound ball attached to a steel wire with a handle. The object is to grasp the hammer by the handle and heave it as far as possible. It is a very difficult feat that takes great strength.

Jim watched as one of the fellows succeeded in throwing the hammer 140 feet—almost half the length of a football field. He studied the proper technique used by the others—then took a shot at it himself. On his first try, Jim successfully threw the hammer 145 feet. The other athletes looked at him as if he were from another planet.

Jim Thorpe seemed to be an athlete who could shine in any sport. He was an outstanding basketball and lacrosse player. He played major-league baseball as well as professional football. His dazzling versatility in track and field made him one of the most memorable Olympians in history. He was so rugged that when a sportswriter once asked him if he was concerned about getting hurt playing football, Jim could only chuckle. "How could anybody get hurt playing football?" he replied.

"He was a coach's dream," said Glenn "Pop" Warner, Jim's coach at Carlisle. "Jim would watch somebody doing something for several minutes; then he'd try it himself,

On the very first throw of his life, Jim tossed the hammer 145 feet. His throw was 5 feet farther than the best effort of one of his school's varsity hammer-throwers.

and almost right away he was doing it like he'd been doing it all his life." Before long, the hammer-throwers found that out. So did a group of high-jumpers on the Carlisle track team, who were trying to clear the bar at 5 feet 9 inches. Although Jim was not on the team at the time, he stood off to the side and watched as one jumper after another took a flying leap, only to knock the bar to the ground. Finally, Jim asked if he could have a crack at it. He was wearing overalls and sport shoes. The other jumpers couldn't wait for Jim to embarrass himself.

Pacing off his steps, Jim raced toward the bar, planted his foot, and then hurtled himself upward. He cleared the bar easily. He had just set a school record—without getting into track shoes or a uniform.

"I never high-jumped before," Jim said. "But if a horse can jump that high, I guess I can do it, too."

A Team of One?

Jim would go on to become the star of the Carlisle track team. People were raving about his achievements—especially after one meet against Lafayette, a team that was undefeated and thought to be unbeatable.

Lafayette's team had 48 members. One popular story is that Jim showed up for the track competition with just one other schoolmate. The Lafayette coaches and athletes were expecting to see 25 or 30 people from Carlisle. A Lafayette team member approached Jim and asked, "Is this your whole team?"

"Well, no," Jim said. "This little fellow is the student manager."

The story isn't actually the truth. And neither is another account of the same day. In that version, the entire Carlisle group consisted of Thorpe and Coach Warner. A Lafayette coach asked Warner where his team was.

"I never high-jumped before," Jim said. "But if a horse can jump that high, I guess I can do it, too."

"Here it is," Warner said, pointing to Jim.

The fact is, Carlisle had other competitors besides Jim Thorpe that day. But it's not hard to see how legends seem to grow around Jim—and why, that day, people may have mistaken him for a one-man team.

In the high jump that day at Lafayette, the winner was Jim Thorpe. In the broad jump, the winner was Jim Thorpe. The shot put? The high hurdles? Low hurdles? All won by Jim Thorpe. By the time he was finished, the Lafayette unbeaten streak was over.

As the athletes left the field that day, all 48 Lafayette men were shaking their heads in wonder. Before long, the whole world would be marveling, too. The legend of Jim Thorpe was just beginning.

2

A Challenging Childhood

One of the things that set him apart was a strong will that seemed to have no limit.

James Francis Thorpe and his twin brother, Charlie, were born on May 28, 1888, in a cabin in Prague, Oklahoma. Of mostly Indian descent, their parents were Hiram Thorpe and Charlotte View Thorpe. They were part of the American Indian tribe known as the Sac and Fox. Jim's great-great-grandfather, Black Hawk, was among the bravest and most respected of all Sac and Fox Indians. As Jim grew older, he learned more about his famous ancestor. He once said, "I am no more proud of my career as an athlete than I am of the fact that I am a direct descendent of that noble warrior."

Prague, Oklahoma, was a tiny prairie town where people supported themselves by farming and hunting. Hiram Thorpe was a great outdoorsman and a powerful man. Often there would be swimming, running, and wrestling contests among tribe members. More often than not, the winner was "Big Hiram," as most people called him.

Big Hiram taught his son Jim the rugged and demanding skills of the frontier. Jim grew strong as he worked alongside his father, learning to trap, hunt, and rope wild colts. Jim often said that he had never seen another man who could match his father's strength and endurance.

Jim's father, Big Hiram Thorpe, taught his son the skills of the rugged frontier, including how to rope wild colts.

When they were six years old, Jim and Charlie began attending the Sac and Fox reservation school. Because the school was 23 miles away from the Thorpe cabin, the boys slept there during the school year, returning home only for holidays and vacations.

Jim and Charlie Thorpe were not only twins, but they were great companions and best friends. They played games together. They studied together. Charlie was no match for Jim's strength and athletic ability. But the brothers had great fun just the same—wrestling, racing, competing at just about everything.

A Family Tragedy

One day, when the boys were eight, Charlie came down with a severe cold. He had chills, a cough, and persistent aches and pains. When the boy didn't get better, Big Hiram and Charlotte became alarmed. It turned out that little Charlie's cold had developed into pneumonia. Today, there are powerful medicines that fight this illness. But in 1896, no such remedies existed. Charlie Thorpe died that year.

Jim was devastated. It was all so sudden. He didn't understand how such a thing could happen. It didn't seem fair. How could his twin brother be healthy enough to wrestle with him one day and be gravely ill such a short time later? As much fun as he had had as a youngster, Jim learned at an early age that life could also be very sad. This was a painful lesson Jim would learn again before he got much older.

Young Jim was devastated by the sudden loss of his twin brother, Charlie.

Jim returned to the reservation school after Charlie's death, but it wasn't the same. He missed his brother terribly. Everywhere he looked at the school, there were reminders of Charlie.

Finally, one morning, young Jim walked out of the school. He didn't tell any teachers or classmates. He just took off— and kept going, sometimes walking briskly, other times running. Twenty-three miles later, Jim arrived home in Prague.

Big Hiram was startled to see his son. He listened to the boy plead his case to stay home and help out on the farm. But nothing Jim said would make Big Hiram change his mind. The Thorpes believed strongly that an education was the key to a better future. Although he was impressed by Jim's strong will, Big Hiram turned Jim around and went with him back to school. The father said good-bye to his son, then started for home.

Jim waited until his father was out of sight. Then the rebellious youngster took

off again. He took a shortcut that shaved miles off the trip. It was a rough, unused road, but it was worth it. Jim was determined not only to get home, but also to beat his father there. Jim ran and ran, keeping up a steady pace. By the time Big Hiram lumbered into the front yard, Jim was standing there, waiting for him. Big Hiram wouldn't have been much more surprised if he'd seen a herd of flying cows.

A New School and a New Friend

This now turned into a battle of wills. But Big Hiram was not going to lose. The only answer, he figured, was to ship his son to a school so far away that Jim couldn't think about getting home on foot. Jim's next school address became Lawrence, Kansas, where he attended an American Indian school known as the Haskell Institute.

Jim wound up staying at Haskell for four years. He liked the school, and he made many new friends. One of them, a young man named Chauncey Archiquette, was the top athlete at the school. Chauncey was especially good at baseball and football, games that Jim did not get to play back on the reservation.

Chauncey was a likable kid and a very good teacher. Jim would constantly ask him questions, but Chauncey never seemed to tire of answering them. He always encouraged Jim to keep working to get better at the games. "Try it yourself! And practice a lot!" These were Chauncey's constant words of advice.

Jim's natural gifts made him a quick learner. Following the guidance of his friend, he became a skillful athlete. One of the things that set him apart from the other boys was a strong will that seemed to have no limit. When young Jim felt challenged, and when he set his mind to accomplish a certain feat, he would do whatever was necessary to succeed.

Another Loss

In 1900, Jim received word that his father had been injured in a hunting accident. Worried and upset, Jim jumped a freight train and headed home. When he arrived, he found his father well on the way to recovery. But shortly after Jim's arrival, his mother developed a blood disorder. Charlotte View Thorpe never got over the ailment. She died right there on the family farm. Jim was only 12 years old.

Several years passed, and Jim found himself growing up quickly. There were times when he had arguments with his father. Both of them felt great sorrow over losing Charlotte.

A Thirst for Adventure

After his mother died, Jim left home for a while, headed for Texas, and managed to support himself for close to a year. When Jim returned home, Big Hiram felt a surge of pride in his son. He could see that young Jim had not only a strong body but a strong will as well. Big Hiram noticed that when Jim was in a difficult spot, it only made him work harder to get out of it.

As he grew up, Jim developed a thirst for adventure. He feared almost nothing.

Another quality appeared in the young Jim. He loved adventure. He feared almost nothing. Whether it was trotting 23 miles home from school or taking off for Texas, he had a thirst for excitement.

In 1903, an unexpected visitor stopped by the Sac and Fox reservation. The man was an official of the Carlisle Indian School, located in southern Pennsylvania. The official was looking for students for the school. He told Jim and Big Hiram about the instruction the school offered in different trades. It appealed to Big Hiram, who wanted Jim to get the proper schooling. And it appealed to Jim—the adventure of going to a new, faraway place. Soon Jim was leaving Oklahoma and heading east. He didn't know it then, but neither he, nor Carlisle, would ever be the same.

3

Building a Reputation

"Here was the theoretical superplayer in flesh and blood."

The Carlisle School in Pennsylvania was founded by an army officer, Lieutenant Richard Henry Pratt, who had fought in the Civil War. He had received honors and had traveled through a good portion of the country. He came to know a number of Indians from a variety of different tribes.

In the late 1800s, there were many conflicts between white people and Native Americans. Because they had lived on the land before white people, many Native Americans were deeply upset that their land was being taken away from them. Some Indian tribes fought hard to hold on to their territory.

A widespread notion among some white people at the time was that Native Americans were a violent, wild group. Many whites also felt that they couldn't be trusted and were not smart enough to learn a more civilized way of living. But Lieutenant Pratt knew that this was not true. Lieutenant Pratt felt it was wrong to make generalizations about an entire group of people. He felt Native Americans deserved an opportunity for schooling, to learn trades, the same as anybody else.

It took several years of badgering, but Lieutenant Pratt finally persuaded government officials to go along with his idea. He was given an old army barracks in Carlisle, Pennsylvania. After countless hours of repairing and rebuilding, the ramshackle barracks came back to life. The Carlisle School opened in 1879.

The school was well established by the time Jim Thorpe enrolled in 1908. Jim was just beginning his new life at Carlisle, when one of his teachers pulled him aside. For a moment, Jim thought he had done something wrong or was going to get a stern lecture about studying harder. But the news was much sadder than that. Jim's father had just died. He had fallen victim to .a blood disorder, the same illness that had claimed the life of Jim's mother.

Jim was almost getting used to tragedy by now, but the loss of his father was still a crushing blow. Jim was never one to show much emotion. He kept most of the grief he felt bottled up inside. It left Jim with a hurt, hollow feeling to think that he would never go hunting or horseback riding with his father again. The man Jim admired above all others was now gone, just as his twin brother and his mother were gone.

The Carlisle School in the hills of Pennsylvania was created to offer Native Americans a good education.

Meanwhile, young Jim was rapidly growing up. Upon his arrival in Pennsylvania, Jim was a slightly built lad, barely five feet tall and weighing not much more than 100 pounds. But in just a few years, he sprouted into a powerful six-footer who weighed 185 pounds.

While at the school, Jim chose to study to be a tailor. When he wasn't learning about stitching clothes, he was often out on the playing fields. Carlisle had a reputation for having fine athletic teams. The school also had intramural leagues, in which students would play among themselves. It was in these leagues that Jim first started playing.

Becoming a "Hotshot"

There was a tailors' team in the intramural football league, and muscular young Jim

was assigned to play guard. It is a position that requires great strength and blocking ability. Jim had both, and he excelled as guard. His performance caught the eye of the coach of the school's reserve team— the backups to the Carlisle varsity. The reserves were called the "Hotshots." When the Hotshot coach asked Jim if he wanted to join them, the youngster didn't hesitate.

Jim played almost everything. Before he was finished at Carlisle, he earned varsity letters in 11 sports.

The school had another coach as well. His name was Glenn "Pop" Warner. Known throughout the college sports world as a brilliant coach, Warner had trained some of Carlisle's finest athletes. It didn't take long for Jim to grab Pop Warner's attention. The famous coach had already discovered Jim's jumping ability by accident. Coach Warner happened to be watching the day Jim soared over the high bar in his overalls. When Pop saw that, he needed no further convincing. He asked Jim to join the track team in 1909.

Then came another accident. Coach Warner was at the edge of the practice field, when suddenly he noticed a football flying through the air as if it had been shot from a cannon. The stunned coach looked over and saw Jim Thorpe—again in work clothes. Jim had been walking by the field, saw some footballs lying around, and figured he'd boot a few. Such talent could not go to waste, coach Warner told himself.

Soon Jim was a Carlisle football player as well as a Carlisle track man. In fact, he played almost everything before he was finished. He earned a varsity letter in 11 sports. Jim had such good coordination that he even learned ballroom dancing. Nobody was surprised when Jim later wound up as a champion dancer! In 1912, he won the intercollegiate ballroom dancing championship.

Coach Warner asked Jim to join the Carlisle football team after he saw Jim kick a football like a rocket on the playing field one day.

A Big Chance

Jim's first big football opportunity came in a game against Pennsylvania, a fine team from the Ivy League. Albert Payne, a star halfback for Carlisle, suffered a knee injury and was forced to leave the game. Pop Warner needed a replacement. He called in Jim Thorpe.

The team put him right to work. The quarterback handed off to Jim, who tucked the ball next to his body—and then was soundly slammed by what felt like the entire Penn team. There were no holes to find; there was no chance to go anywhere. Jim lost yardage on the play, but now he really burned with determination.

On the next handoff, Jim bulled right through the line. He knocked over who-ever was in his path and slipped by a few others. He broke into the open and burst past every Penn player. Nobody was going to catch him. Jim ran 75 yards for a touchdown. And in the end zone, his overjoyed teammates mobbed him. Jim was the star of the day.

As a runner, Jim had a unique combina-tion of speed and strength. He could run through tacklers as well as run away from them. He was a superb field-goal kicker and punter. On defense, he used his power to deliver jarring tackles to opponents.

With Jim leading the way, the little Indian school, with just one thousand students, became a fearsome football machine. Carlisle was a match for even the biggest and most famous college teams. In 1911, Carlisle even defeated Harvard, the defending national champion. The final score was 18 to 15. Jim Thorpe not only kicked four field goals, but he also scored his team's touchdown—worth five points in those days. Perry Haughton, the Harvard coach, had seen quite enough.

"Watching him turn the ends, slash off, tackle, kick, and pass the tackle, I realized that here was the theoretical superplayer in flesh and blood," the Harvard coach said.

A "Tour" with the Army

The performance against Harvard was nothing compared with what Jim did against Army, another eastern powerhouse. Army's players were tough, strong, and well drilled. The cadet defense was as hard to break as a stone wall.

During the Army game, Carlisle had the ball deep in its own territory. Taking the handoff at his 8-yard line, Jim exploded through a hole and outraced everybody all the way down the field for a touchdown. It was a breathtaking 92-yard run—except that an official had thrown a flag on the

play. The penalty canceled the touchdown. The ball was brought all the way back to the Carlisle three-yard line.

So what did Jim Thorpe do? He got the ball again on the next play—and this time galloped 97 yards for a touchdown! One of the Army stars was a rugged fellow named Dwight Eisenhower, who would one day become president of the United States. On that afternoon, young Dwight and his fellow cadets were totally frustrated. They couldn't stop Jim, who sparked a 27-to-6 victory by scoring every Carlisle point—two touchdown runs, a touchdown pass, three field goals, and three extra points.

"I've just officiated at a game in which I've seen the greatest football player ever," one referee said.

Jim finished the season with national college records of 25 touchdowns and 198 points and was chosen as an All-American halfback for both 1911 and, later, 1912. After one of Jim's brilliant performances, one of the officials was left almost speechless. "I've just officiated at a game in which I've seen the greatest football player ever," he said.

Jim continued to excel at other sports, too. On the Carlisle baseball team, he was a dangerous home-run hitter, a fine fielder, and a pitcher with a blazing fastball. The Pittsburgh Pirates were so impressed by him that one spring they sent a scout to

Carlisle to sign him up. The scout had a blank check in his hand. He told Jim he could fill in the number he wanted. Jim, however, wasn't ready to leave Carlisle, so he declined the generous offer.

A Brief Vacation

Between 1909 and 1910, Jim took some time away from school. He wanted a break, and he also needed to earn a little money. When some of his friends told him about an opportunity to try out for a minor-league baseball team in Rocky Mount, North Carolina, Jim was excited. Other college stars from around the country also played in the league. Jim went to North Carolina, made the team, and performed exceptionally well.

During his time away, Jim received a letter from Pop Warner, who suggested that he return to Carlisle to begin training for the greatest competition of all: the Olympic Games. In fact, Pop thought that Jim's all-around skill would make him a natural for the decathlon—a grueling competition of 10 events. The winner of the decathlon is often regarded as the world's greatest athlete.

Jim returned to Carlisle and began looking forward to what would be his greatest adventure yet.

4

An Olympic Triumph

"When Jim looked up, there were 60,000 people cheering."

It took Jim no time at all to get back into the swing of things at Carlisle. He enjoyed so much success on Pop Warner's track team that he couldn't wait for the Olympics to begin. He would have a chance to test his skill and strength against the leading athletes from around the world.

Jim felt so confident that he told Coach Warner he didn't want to enter just the decathlon. He also wanted to compete in the pentathlon—another exhausting event made up of five separate competitions. In the pentathlon, athletes are ranked according to their performance in the long jump, the javelin throw, the 200-meter hurdles, the 1,500-meter run, and the discus throw. Jim also qualified for the individual long-jump and high-jump events. With the 10 events of the decathlon, there was no doubt that Jim was going to be the busiest man in all of Stockholm, Sweden.

Across the Sea

The American Olympic team took a giant ocean liner, *The Finland,* to get to the Olympic Games. Because it was a long trip, the athletes made sure to keep up their training so that they would be in peak condition upon arriving in Sweden.

The one exception was Jim Thorpe. Jim spent most of his time in a deck chair with his eyes closed. He didn't mean to show up the other athletes. It was just that Jim felt that he was in supreme condition already. Having played so many sports at Carlisle for so long, Jim believed the best thing he could do was to relax. While he was in his chair, he would go over different events in his mind. He would imagine exactly what he had to do to perform well. Once the team arrived in Stockholm, Jim switched his chair for a hammock, and he kept on resting. He really believed that his stategy would give him the energy and the sharp mental focus that he would need in the up-coming competition.

One man who wasn't buying Jim's training approach was Mike Murphy, the coach of the American team. Coach Murphy was a long-time instructor who was known as a strict task-master. The Carlisle Indian was not exactly Murphy's idea of a dedicated athlete. In fact, Coach Murphy decided that Jim was one of the laziest men he'd ever seen.

Jim decided to compete in the pentathlon, the decathlon, and two individual competitions— a total of 17 events.

One day, an angry Murphy approached Pop Warner. "Glenn, I've seen some queer birds in my day, but your Indian beats all!" Murphy declared. "I don't see him do anything but sleep!"

Pop Warner tried to settle Coach Murphy down. "Don't worry, Mike," Pop said. "All those two-for-a-nickel events you've got lined up for Thorpe won't bother him. He's in shape. What with football, lacrosse, baseball, and track back at school, how could he be out of shape? This sleeping is the best training ever—for Jim."

Finally—The Games

Whatever concerns Coach Murphy may have had did not last long once the 1912 Olympics began. The pentathlon was held on the first full day of competition. Before a jam-packed crowd, Jim began his pursuit of his first Olympic medal. He began the event by winning the long jump with a leap of 23 feet 2 inches. After that, he won the discus throw, followed by the 1,500-meter run. He placed third in the javelin throw, but he more than made up for that in the 200-meter hurdles, which he ran in somebody else's shoes!

Shortly before the race, Jim couldn't find his spiked hurdling shoes. He and Pop Warner looked everywhere, but there was just no time to search for them. Jim needed shoes—and fast. Scurrying back into the locker room, Pop and Jim came across a pair of sprinter's shoes. To make them suitable for hurdling, Pop quickly hammered extra spikes into the heels.

Jim's confidence was so high that he wasn't going to let these strange shoes bother him. In the 200-meter hurdles, he outran fellow American, James Donahue, to capture another first place. Jim won the pentathlon, but more than that, he so dominated the event that one writer called it "no contest at all . . . just as easy for Jim as picking strawberries out of a dish."

Jim's strawberry picking was just beginning. His performance in the pentathlon was the talk of the Olympics. When the decathlon came around, the question that everybody was asking was, "Can the Carlisle Indian do it again?"

In the decathlon, Jim had twice as many events to compete in. There was tremendous pressure on him to repeat his heroics. What's more, he had never competed in a decathlon before.

But if tiredness and high hopes were problems, nobody ever would have known it by watching Jim in the decathlon. Jim swept the competition by placing first in the 110-meter hurdles and by winning the high jump, the 1,500-meter run, and the shot put. These wins were followed by four third-place finishes in other events, and two fourth-place finishes. In 10 events against the finest athletes from all corners of the globe, Jim Thorpe set a world record by earning 8,412 points. The second-place finisher, Hugo Wieslander of Sweden, performed splendidly himself. Yet Wieslander was almost 700 points behind the great Jim Thorpe.

The World's Greatest Athlete

Jim's feats in Stockholm made him the most famous athlete in the world. Indeed, they made him one of the most famous *people* in the world. On the victory stand, Jim Thorpe was given his two precious gold medals as the flag of the United States flapped high overhead. Sweden's King Gustav V asked the heroic Sac and Fox Indian to step

Opposite:
The Olympic decathlon is a competition made up of 10 separate events: the 100-meter dash, the long jump, the shot put, the high jump, the 400-meter run, the discus throw, the 110-meter hurdles, the pole vault, the javelin throw, and the 1,500-meter run. In 1912, Jim swept the competition with a world record total of 8,412 points.

31

forward. The king handed Jim a glittering statue covered with valuable jewels. This was a gift from the leader of Russia, the king explained. He also handed Jim a bronze bust of himself, another keepsake of Jim's heroic visit to Sweden. When Jim looked up, there were 60,000 people cheering. The crowd seemed to reach all the way up to the sky. It was a spectacle he could hardly believe.

After Jim's Olympic triumphs, he was honored at a ceremony by Sweden's King Gustav V, who said that Jim was the "greatest athlete in the world." More than 60,000 people gathered to cheer Jim at the ceremony.

(Continued on page 49)

1912

STOCKHOLM, SWEDEN

School Days

As a teenager, Jim enrolled at the Carlisle Indian School in Pennsylvania. The school, which was founded by army officer Lieutenant Richard Henry Pratt in 1879, was created especially for Native Americans. While attending Carlisle, Jim's natural athletic ability was quickly noticed by the teaching staff, and he soon became one of the school's star athletes. *Below:* The Carlisle School was converted from an old army barracks that was used during the Civil War. *Right*: An early portrait of Jim during his Carlisle days.

STAR ATHLETE

Once Jim's natural athletic ability was recognized by his school's coach, Pop Warner, Jim was asked to play on a number of the Carlisle teams. It seemed that, no matter what Jim played, he became a star. All in all, Jim earned a varsity letter in 11 sports. *Above:* Jim (back row, center) poses for a group portrait with Carlisle's championship track team. (Pop Warner stands next to him in the jacket and tie.) *Right*: Jim's kicking ability became legendary in the college football world. In one game against Harvard, Jim kicked four field goals and scored the winning touchdown. *Below:* Carlisle's champion football team; Jim is in the back row, far right. *Opposite*: Jim after a shot-put throw in a college competition.

37

THE GAMES IN STOCKHOLM

During the Olympic Games in Stockholm, Sweden, in 1912, Jim competed in a number of events, including both the pentathlon and the decathlon. The first full day of Olympic competition was filled with the pentathlon—five separate events made up of the broad jump, the discus throw, the 1,500-meter run, the javelin throw, and the hurdles. Two months before the Games, Jim had never thrown a javelin in his life. Nevertheless, he succeeded in placing second in the event. *Right:* Jim began the 1912 pentathlon with a winning broad jump of 23 feet 2 inches. *Below:* After winning the discus throw, Jim won the 1,500-meter run. Here, he crouches in his starting position.

LIKE "PICKING STRAWBERRIES OUT OF A DISH"

Jim finished the 1912 pentathlon by running away with first place in the 200-meter hurdles (*shown here*). The great Thorpe had so dominated the competition that he instantly became the talk of the Stockholm Games. One sportswriter wrote of the pentathlon that it was "no contest at all...just as easy for Jim as picking strawberries out of a dish."

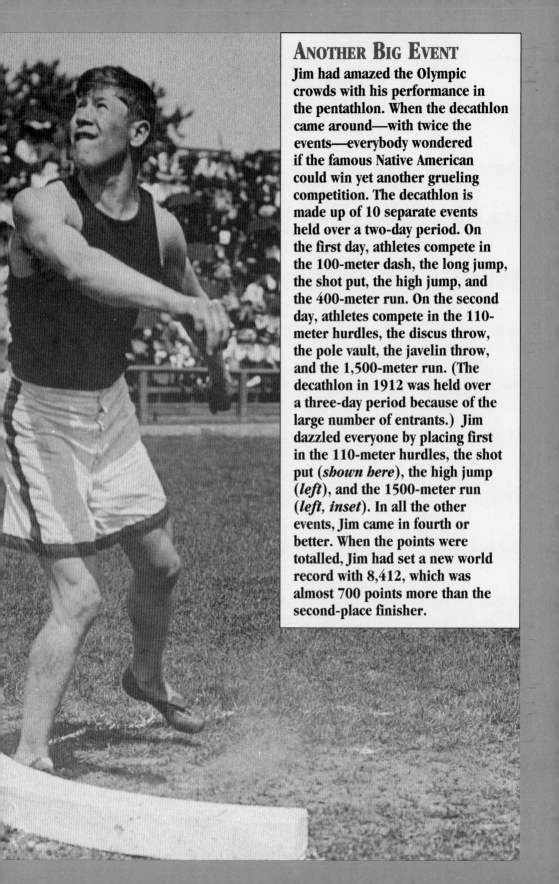

ANOTHER BIG EVENT

Jim had amazed the Olympic crowds with his performance in the pentathlon. When the decathlon came around—with twice the events—everybody wondered if the famous Native American could win yet another grueling competition. The decathlon is made up of 10 separate events held over a two-day period. On the first day, athletes compete in the 100-meter dash, the long jump, the shot put, the high jump, and the 400-meter run. On the second day, athletes compete in the 110-meter hurdles, the discus throw, the pole vault, the javelin throw, and the 1,500-meter run. (The decathlon in 1912 was held over a three-day period because of the large number of entrants.) Jim dazzled everyone by placing first in the 110-meter hurdles, the shot put (*shown here*), the high jump (*left*), and the 1500-meter run (*left, inset*). In all the other events, Jim came in fourth or better. When the points were totalled, Jim had set a new world record with 8,412, which was almost 700 points more than the second-place finisher.

WORLD-FAMOUS SUPERSTAR

Jim's amazing performance in Stockholm made him the world's most famous athlete. After he was honored at a special ceremony by King Gustav V of Sweden, Jim returned to the United States as a national hero. While he was strolling down New York City's Broadway during a ticker-tape parade in his honor, Jim was awed by his country's show of appreciation. Later, he recalled, "I heard people yelling my name—and I couldn't realize how one fellow could have so many friends." *Above:* Jim is given an Olympic homecoming at the Carlisle School. On the left is Pop Warner, and shaking hands with Jim is the school's president and fellow classmate of Jim's, Mr. Tewanima. *Right*: In 1913, Jim married Iva Miller in a small ceremony, just before he started his professional baseball career with the New York Giants. *Inset, right*: Jim sits with his first-born son, Jim Jr., who died in 1917 from infantile paralysis.

LIFE AS A PROFESSIONAL ATHLETE

In 1913, Jim signed with the New York Giants baseball team for an annual salary of $6,000. A number of other professional teams had wanted him, but Jim thought playing for a New York team would be the most exciting. *Right*: Jim's natural abilities served him well as both a fielder and a hitter. *Above, left to right*: The New York Giants batting order in 1915: Snodgrass, Doyle, Lobert, Fletcher, Mertle, Burns, Thorpe, Murray, and Meyers. After 6 years in baseball, Jim decided to move over to his preferred sport of football. His professional career in football would span another 15 years and would bring him even more popularity than his baseball years.

THE LATER YEARS

Once his career as a professional athlete was over, Jim faced hard times, both personally and professionally. Although he managed to pick up occasional work as an actor in Hollywood and as a performer at athletic exhibitions, Jim did not prosper. Despite his hard luck, the world never stopped acknowledging that Jim was the greatest athlete of the twentieth century. Here, the 61-year-old Jim poses with his eldest son, Phil, at a dinner honoring the great Olympian. Jim died of a heart attack three years later.

(Continued from page 32)

"You, sir, are the greatest athlete in the world," King Gustav told him.

"Thanks, King," Jim Thorpe replied, not knowing what else to say.

Not surprisingly, Jim returned to the United States as one of the greatest heroes the country had ever known. People mobbed him everywhere he went. In New York City, a ticker-tape parade was held in his honor. As the caravan moved down Broadway, hundreds of thousands of people showered him with affection. People chanted his name. There were similar honors in Philadelphia and Boston. Jim was astounded. It was as if the whole country were reaching out to hug him.

"I heard people yelling my name, and I couldn't realize how one fellow could have so many friends," he said later.

It was probably the most glorious homecoming an American athlete ever had.

Jim went back to Carlisle to finish his schooling. That fall, there were more great efforts on the football field. He was the biggest name in sports, a beloved figure.

What Jim didn't know was that the greatest time of his life would come to a crashing halt before his medals were even six months old. Jim Thorpe would be back in the headlines, but this time, it would leave him a bitter, lonely man.

5

Misfortune

***His hurt was so deep that he felt
almost numb.***

In 1913, still happy from his great triumphs, Jim married his first wife, Iva Miller. But their lives together would not be happy for very long. Late in January of 1913, a gripping and startling newspaper report rocked the entire sports world. The report said that Jim Thorpe, Olympic hero, had once played baseball for money in Rocky Mount, North Carolina. If this report was true, it meant that Jim's status as an amateur was in serious danger. It even meant that Olympic officials might have the power to strip him of his gold medals.

The moment he heard the news, Pop Warner sat down with his famous pupil.

Jim told the coach that it was true. He had played ball for two summers. He was paid $25 per week. But Jim could not believe that this would lead people to consider him a professional athlete. As far as he was concerned, this was just another in a series of temporary jobs he had taken while at Carlisle. He had worked in a kitchen. He had worked on a farm. In North Carolina, he had played ball. He loved playing ball. Why not earn a little spending money doing something he loved?

The fact was that many college players competed in the minor league; but they did not lose their amateur standing. The difference was that the others played under phony names. To avoid trouble, these players simply hid their true identities. This way, they could go back to their colleges and continue to play as amateurs. Jim knew little of the official rules and regulations of amateur sports or of the Olympics. He saw no reason to change his name. When they asked who he was, he told them: James Thorpe. That was how his name appeared in the box scores.

The American Athletic Union (A.A.U.) began investigating the matter. All over the country, sportswriters and fans said it was unfair and cruel to take Jim's accomplishments away because of a minor mistake.

With so much experience in athletics, Pop Warner did all he could to help. Pop and Jim wrote long letters to the A.A.U. After the Olympics, many companies and organizations approached Jim, offering great sums of money. Jim turned them all down. He wanted to go back to Carlisle. When pro scouts came around to try to sign him, they all considered him an amateur. Almost everyone did.

Pleading His Case

Jim apologized for his mistake. He said he meant nobody any harm. He didn't try to mislead anybody. In his letter to James E. Sullivan, chairman of the A.A.U., Jim wrote, "I hope I will be partly excused by the fact that I was simply an Indian schoolboy and did not know all about such things. . . . I was not very wise to the ways of the world and did not realize that this was wrong and it made me a professional in track sports. . . ."

The A.A.U. considered the case carefully. American officials met with executives of the International Olympic Committee, which supervises the Olympics. Despite the tremendous outpouring of support for Jim, the decision was that he was a professional athlete when he competed in the Olympics. Therefore, his records would be erased from the books. His gold medals did not belong to him anymore and had to be returned. It was as if Jim Thorpe had never been to Stockholm at all . . . as if King Gustav had never hailed him as the greatest athlete in the world.

Jim Thorpe was crushed. His hurt was so deep that he felt almost numb. He had won those Olympic events. How could they take his medals away?

On a gloomy day in February, 1913, Jim and Pop Warner gathered his medals and trophies and carted them to the post office

Despite all their efforts, Jim and Pop Warner could not convince the International Olympic Committee to allow Jim to keep his medals. In February 1913, only a few months after he had won the pentathlon and decathlon, Jim and Pop packed up the medals and sent them back to the Olympic officials.

in Carlisle. Jim felt as though he were mailing off parts of himself.

The Olympic officials announced they would award Jim's gold medals to the second-place finishers in the decathlon and pentathlon. The runners-up were Hugo Wieslander of Sweden and Ferdinand Bie of Norway.

But neither man would accept his award because each did not feel he had earned it.

After hearing about the International Olympic Committee's decision, Hugo Wieslander of Sweden said, "I didn't win the Olympic decathlon. James Thorpe did."

Wieslander never even opened the package when it arrived at his home. He just wrote on the outside, "I didn't win the Olympic decathlon. James Thorpe did." These gestures didn't take away the sting of Jim's hurt, but they helped. Although Jim didn't have the medals anymore, he still had plenty of supporters.

6

The End of a Legend

Jim never found the success off the field that he enjoyed on it.

Jim Thorpe did his best to put the decision by the A.A.U. behind him. There was nothing to be done to change anyone's mind now.

A number of major-league baseball teams wanted Jim to play for them. In 1913, he signed with the New York Giants for an annual salary of $6,000. The Giants manager was a small, crusty man named John McGraw, who ruled over his players with an iron hand. McGraw's nickname was "Little Napoleon." John McGraw was happy about acquiring the famous Olympian. But the good feelings did not last for long. Jim Thorpe and John McGraw did not get along at all.

Jim was with the Giants until 1919, except for a season with the Cincinnati Reds. Although he had flashes of excellence, Jim was never a regular player. It made him angry that the manager wouldn't give him a full chance. It made McGraw just as angry that Jim did not seem to be a dedicated, hardworking player. The Thorpe-McGraw combination never improved.

Things in Jim's personal life had not been much better, either. But by far the most tragic blow was when Jim Jr., the first child of Jim and his first wife, Iva, died of infantile paralysis in 1917. The child was just four years old. Jim had experienced losses his whole life, starting with his twin brother, but the grief of losing a child was almost unbearable.

The truth is that football was always a sport Jim preferred anyway. There was something about the aggressiveness and the contact of the gridiron that got his juices going. Jim's pro-football career eventually spanned 15 years.

But in 1919, the National Football League (NFL) was just starting out. Jim played a big role in getting the newly formed NFL off the ground. In 1920, in fact, he was named president of professional football. Having a big name like Jim Thorpe in charge gave the game a mighty boost.

Over the years, Jim played on many different teams. His favorite was a club called the Oorang Indians. Based in Ohio, the Oorang team was made up entirely of players of Indian descent. Jim put together a fine collection of talent, including a couple of other former Carlisle stars, including Joe Guyon and Elmer Busch. Jim often said that the Oorang Indians was the finest pro team he had ever seen.

Like many athletes, Jim had a difficult time when he stopped playing.

By the time Jim retired in 1929, pro football was on its way toward success. For all his contributions, both on the field and off, Jim Thorpe was later inducted into the Professional Football Hall of Fame.

Off the Field

Like many athletes, Jim had a difficult time when he stopped playing. Professional athletes start playing games early in their lives. Often, they don't really know much about anything else. Then they suddenly have to find another means of supporting themselves and their families. The transition isn't always easy, especially for those who do not have a good education.

In 1926, Jim married for the second time. His wife was Frieda Kirkpatrick, a Scotch-Irish woman and the daughter of a golf-club manager. Together, Jim and Frieda had

57

four children, all boys—Phil, Bill, Dick, and Jack. Jim was happy for a while, but in other areas he was struggling.

For Jim, the sad fact is that he never found the success off the field that he enjoyed on it. He didn't have any special skills that would help him get steady work. And he wasn't experienced in the business world. When the United States sank into the Great Depression in the 1930s, millions of people struggled to find work. That only made things harder for Jim.

Jim bounced from state to state, and from job to job. He worked in the field of recreation. He worked as a security guard. He tried painting. He even got some small parts in Hollywood films. But nothing seemed to last, and the longer he struggled, the more Jim felt dissatisfied and unhappy.

In the early 1930s, Jim took a job in California digging ditches. It was strenuous labor, and it paid him only four dollars per day. When the 1932 Los Angeles Olympics came around, the hero of just 20 years earlier could not even afford a ticket.

A Brief Moment of Glory

There was a huge outpouring from people all over the country when they heard of Jim Thorpe's plight. Even people Jim had never met sympathized with him. One of those in attendance in Los Angeles was Charles Curtis, vice-president of the United States. Curtis, who was part Indian, invited Jim Thorpe to sit with him in the vice-president's special box. When Jim Thorpe's presence was announced to the massive crowd in the Los Angeles Coliseum, there was a long, loud ovation. Everywhere Jim looked, people were cheering for him. It was a great feeling, knowing people had not forgotten him.

His Olympic ovation, however, provided only temporary relief for Jim Thorpe. His difficulties continued. One of his biggest problems was drinking. More and more,

When it was announced at the 1932 Games in Los Angeles that Jim Thorpe was in the audience, the massive crowd rose to its feet and gave him a long and loud standing ovation.

Jim turned to alcohol to feel better, but it only made his unhappiness worse. Jim was convinced that he needed alcohol to get by. But the fact was that it added to his burden tremendously. In fact, his health began to worsen. He served his country, enlisting in the merchant marine in 1945. But for Jim, fulfillment was almost impossible to achieve and maintain.

Then he developed cancer and had to have an operation. Soon after that, he suffered a heart attack, his second. Jim and his third wife—Patricia Askew, whom he had married in 1945—hoped that Jim's health would improve.

But on March 28, 1953, shortly after dinner, Jim Thorpe felt a sharp pain in his chest. He slumped to the floor, a victim of yet another heart attack. This one was too severe to recover from, even for an old Sac and Fox warrior. Jim Thorpe was dead at the age of 64.

The one thing that would have meant more to Jim than anything—the return of his Olympic medals—did not happen in his lifetime. People made many efforts on his behalf, and various officials and politicians argued his case before the International Olympic Committee.

It wasn't until October 13, 1982, that the International Olympic Committee finally

listened to reason. After weighing the evidence once more, the officials voted to return the medals to the man who had won them, Jim Thorpe. At a special ceremony on January 18, 1983, Jim's gold medals were presented to his children. The children, who were all adults by then, were deeply moved by the gesture. Jim's family also felt deep sadness, because, for the great Jim Thorpe, the return of his precious medals came 30 years too late.

In October 1982, the International Olympic Committee finally agreed to return Jim Thorpe to his rightful place in Olympic history. At a special ceremony, Jim Thorpe's gold medals were presented to his children.

Glossary

ancestor A person who is related by heritage to another person or group of people.

decathlon An athletic competition, usually held over two days, made up of 10 separate events: the 100-meter dash, the long jump, the shot put, the high jump, the 400-meter run, the discus throw, the 110-meter hurdles, the pole vault, the javelin throw, and the 1,500-meter run.

discus A disk that is thicker in the middle than around the edges; thrown for distance in athletic competition.

hammer A 16-pound ball attached to a steel wire that is thrown for distance in athletic competition.

infantile paralysis An often fatal disease that is characterized by fever, paralysis, and the breakdown of muscles.

intramural Occurring within a particular school or organization; often refers to athletic teams or groups.

javelin A slender spear, about 8 1/2 feet (2.6 meters) long, that is thrown in athletic competition.

merchant marines A group of people who work and sail on commercial ships for a particular nation.

pentathlon An athletic competition made up of five separate events: the long jump, the discus throw, the 1,500-meter run, the javelin throw, and the 200-meter hurdles.

shot put A field event in which an iron ball is thrown for distance.

For Further Reading

Arnold, Caroline. *The Olympic Summer Games*. New York: Franklin Watts, 1991.

Duden, Jane. *The Olympics*. New York: Crestwood House, 1991.

Jarrett, William. *Timetables of Sports History: The Olympic Games*. New York: Facts On File, 1990.

Merrison, Tim. *Field Athletics*. New York: Crestwood House, 1991.

Rivinus, Edward F. *Jim Thorpe*. Milwaukee: Raintree Steck-Vaughn, 1990.

Sandelson, Robert. *Track Athletics*. New York: Crestwood House, 1991.

Tatlow, Peter. *The Olympics*. New York: Franklin Watts, 1988.

Index

Photo Credits

Cover: Courtesy U.S. Olympic Committee; cover detail: AP/Wide World Photos; pp. 33, 39, 46: UPI/Bettman; pp. 34, 36, 37, 43, 44, 45: U.S. Army Military History Institute; pp. 38, 45, 47: Curtis Management Group; p. 42 (with inset): Courtesy U.S. Olympic Committee; p. 47: National Baseball Library, Cooperstown, NY; pp. 4, 48: AP/Wide World Photos.